ENTRY TO THE TRAITORS' GATE

SPECTACULAR
LONDON

Text by

Julian Shuckburgh

Photography by

Axiom Photographic Agency

Photographers

Ian Cumming

Alberto Arzoz

Steve Benbow

Joe Beynon

C Bowman

Vicki Couchman

Richard Crawford

Renzo Frontoni

Brian Harris

Doug McKinlay

James Morris

Chris Parker

Paul Quayle

Simon Roberts

Ellen Rooney

Eitan Simanor

Anna Watson

Alan Williams

DUNCAN BAIRD PUBLISHERS

LONDON

Spectacular London

Researched, compiled, edited and designed by Duncan Baird Publishers, London.

Copyright © 2005 Hugh Lauter Levin Associates, Inc.
Text copyright © Julian Shuckburgh
Photographs © Axiom Photographic Agency

ISBN 1-84483-136-1

Printed in Hong Kong

All photographs supplied by Axiom Photographic Agency except the following
The Royal Collection © HM Queen Elizabeth II: 52–53, 113; The Bridgeman Art Library: 28 (British
Library), 26, 32 (Guildhall Library, Corporation of London), 29 (Museum of Fine Arts, Budapest), 30
(Collection of the Earl of Pembroke, Wilton House), 27 (Christopher Wood), 31 (Yale Center for British
Art, Paul Mellon Collection); Camera Press/Mark Shenley: 48; Corbis: 20, 23/Alan Woolfitt; Illustrated
London News Picture Library: 33; ImageState: 120–122; Imperial War Museum, London: 112; The
Natural History Museum, London: 104; The Ritz Hotel, London: 126.

PAGE I
THE TOWER OF LONDON
Home of the Crown Jewels, the Tower of London
has been variously a royal palace, a prison,
an arsenal, a mint and a jewel house during its
900-year history.

PREVIOUS PAGES
BUCKINGHAM PALACE
Through the gates in front of Buckingham Palace
we see the state apartments of this grand building,
used by royalty and heads of state, diplomats,
politicians and other invited guests.
plus one line here

THE THAMES FROM WATERLOO
Somerset House faces the river on the far side
of Waterloo Bridge, and beyond it are three ships
docked along Victoria Embankment. The largest
is HQS Wellington, the Headquartership of the
Honourable Company of Master Mariners, which
can be hired out for parties.

SOMERSET HOUSE
For many years Somerset House, on the Strand,
was largely occupied by government departments,
but it has recently been renovated and opened to
the public, and contains the magnificent Courtauld
Institute collection of Old-Master paintings.

ST JAMES'S PARK
Although right in the heart of Westminster, this
beautiful royal park, dating back to Tudor times,
can still convey a soothingly pastoral atmosphere
in the summer.

THE HOUSES OF PARLIAMENT
The seat of the British government as seen from
the surprisingly peaceful pedestrian area of the
Albert Embankment, on the south side of the river.

THIS PAGE: TOP
A GUARDSMAN AND A GENTLEMAN
A guardsman in his ceremonial bearskin helmet
and a gentleman wearing a top hat attend the
annual Trooping the Colour ceremony in honour
of the Queen's birthday.

THIS PAGE: BOTTOM
TELEPHONE BOXES
London used to be awash with its traditional red
telephone boxes, until they were replaced by more
modern designs. However, some still survive, like
these beside St Paul's Cathedral.

CONTENTS

THE CITY AT NIGHT
This striking view from the heart of the ancient
City shows St Paul's Cathedral from the northeast.
The popular Tate Modern art gallery is just across
the river on the South Bank, reached by the
Millennium Bridge, and in the foreground are
Cheapside and the Bank of England offices.

CONTENTS

INTRODUCTION

Although I have lived in London, almost non-stop, for a lifetime, there are many areas and elements in this enormous and ancient city that still surprise me. Some seem new, such as the dramatic influxes of foreign cultures and peoples, the striking post-modern architecture, or the energy and vitality of its population. But most have links and connections with the London whose history stretches back more than two thousand years – the tiny squares and lanes in the City, the extraordinary mass of objects found in the Thames (on display in Tate Britain), or the weird landscape of the Wetlands Centre in Barnes. As Peter Ackroyd says in his excellent book *London The Biography*, "London is so large and so wild that it contains no less than everything". Even if I were to live here twice as long, I would never know it all or feel familiar with all its complexities.

This is what makes London spectacular, not that it has the magnificent 19th-century architecture of Paris's boulevards, or the crumbling medieval structures of Venice, or the massive size of Mexico City or Tokyo. Its strength seems to lie in its long history of surviving catastrophes, rebuilding itself after being burned down by Queen Boudicca in AD60, or in the Great Fire in 1666, or in the blitz of 1941; but always hanging on to the deep roots of its past. When the war-time bomb sites were cleared in the spring of 1946, in places like Chelsea and Cheapside, strange plants grew up in them which hadn't been seen in central London for centuries – wild flowers, ragwort, lilacs, lilies of the valley. If you examine Frans Hogenberg's map of Tudor London, engraved in 1550, it is amazing to see that practically all the streets and squares he shows are still in place, even if the buildings around them have changed

many times over the last half millennium. And it is not just the physical structure that remains so much unchanged. The character of Londoners and their patterns of behaviour echo traditions that go back over many centuries.

There is much talk in the media today about the multiculturalism of modern London, and indeed the quantity of crime in the streets, and the sharp gap between affluence and poverty. But there is nothing remotely modern about any of these topics: they have been endlessly disputed and agonized over throughout London's entire history. For a start there is nothing new about the wide range of racial and cultural communities who live here. London has housed large populations of immigrants from all over the world for many centuries, and indeed greatly benefited and prospered from their presence. Riots and violent demonstrations, often but not always against injustice or oppression, have occurred down the ages, of which some of the most famous are the Peasants' Revolt in 1382, the Gordon Riots in 1780, the racially motivated Notting Hill riots in 1958, and the Poll Tax riots in Trafalgar Square in 1990. Indeed it could be argued that in recent years protests of this kind – such as the Countryside Alliance marches, and the demonstrations in 2003 against the Iraq war – have been unusually peaceful by London standards.

There is clearly nothing new about street crime in a city, or the stories of notorious murders, which are also an intrinsic part of London's history. Undoubtedly the most famous killings are Jack the Ripper's Whitechapel Murders in 1888, perhaps followed by Dr Crippen's killing of his wife Cora in 1910, and the Reginald Christie mass

murders at 10 Rillington Place in Notting Hill in the 1950s. Addiction to drink is something of a London tradition too, although the consumption of gin, a popular rage among the poor throughout the 18th and 19th centuries, has subsided and been replaced by other forms of alcohol and narcotics.

In most large cities the rich and the poor naturally tend to live in separate districts, and this has been broadly true in London, where

the East End was traditionally the home of the labouring masses, and the affluent moved west. But even in the 19th century it became clear that they were far more intermingled than was generally thought. Charles Booth's remarkable 17-year survey of the living conditions of every London street, finally published in 1903, provided a "poverty map" of central London that reveals how very poor people lived in particular streets in affluent

LEFT
THE LIONS OF TRAFALGAR SQUARE
The bronze lions that defend Nelson's monument in Trafalgar Square were designed by Sir Edwin Landseer and erected in 1867. London's current mayor is trying to reduce the square's pigeon population, so far with limited success.

OPPOSITE
BIG BEN
The clock tower at the northern end of the Houses of Parliament is a world-famous symbol of London. The name actually refers to the huge 13½-ton bell inside, which strikes the hours. It was named after Sir Benjamin Hall, First Commissioner of Works when it was hung in 1859.

areas. For example, the whole of Marylebone was home to the "well-to-do middle classes", except for Rathbone Street and Union Street (now called Riding House Street), where lived people he described as "very poor, casual, with chronic want". The poor may be less deprived today than they were a century ago, but they still exist, and some of them still somehow manage to survive in now fashionable areas such as Notting Hill and Fulham. Meanwhile large parts of the East End, which for so long has been the home of the destitute, are today filled with lavish and expensive department buildings and modern housing.

London was always famous for its polluted air, causing the great fogs that 19th-century novelists such as Charles Dickens, Arthur Conan Doyle and Robert Louis Stevenson wrote about so memorably. The fogs had been around since Roman times, aggravated by the development of London's manufacturing in the 18th century and the burning of coal. By the mid-20th century the lethal "smogs" were killing many hundreds of Londoners each year, and legislation was introduced to limit the use of coal, prohibiting its use in "smokeless zones". The air slowly began to improve, and the last great London fog occurred in December 1962. But pollution still exists, albeit less visible, mostly caused by extrusions from the huge expansion of petrol-driven traffic, and much still needs to be done to reach the anti-pollution targets set by the Government and the European Union.

London has always survived, and presumably will continue to do so, despite all these perennial flaws and imperfections, and Londoners will continue to elect mayors and local councils who will seek compromised solutions to them. That is the London way,

and one of the reasons why it remains one of the most alluring and charismatic cities in the world. Twelve million people visit London every year, and hundreds of thousands immigrate annually to live and work here. Many come from Europe, Canada, Australia and New Zealand, but two thirds of them are from Africa, the Middle East, the Indian subcontinent and the Far East. One of London's many spectacular features is how, in almost every region, you encounter so many people from all over the world, speaking all their different languages and dressed in their preferred national attire.

The striking images and scenes depicted in the following pages, collected from some of London's finest photographers vividly portray the astonishing variety and multiplicity of London life. After a brief outline of the city's two-thousand-year history, they focus on the River Thames, the Square Mile where London began, the influence of the monarchy on its architecture and structure, the green spaces and myriads of local regions, the lavish cultural resources, and the daily lives of the seven million inhabitants of spectacular London.

Julian Shuckburgh
London

OPPOSITE
NUMBER 10 DOWNING STREET
This modest front door is the entrance to the British Prime Minister's official residence just off Whitehall. The building is much larger than it appears, and contains the Cabinet Room and numerous offices, as well as the Prime Minister's private apartment.

LEFT
WHITEHALL
Horse Guards, on the eastern side of Horse Guards Parade, is a charming stone building occupied by the Commander-in-Chief of Britain's combined armed forces. Every day two mounted troops of the Life Guards or Royal Horse Guards regiments are posted in front of the building facing Whitehall and the passing traffic. This is a favourite spot for tourists to stand and have their photograph taken, but the guardsmen will never smile for the camera.

OPPOSITE
JUDGES
The House of Lords, the unelected upper House of Parliament, is unique in combining both legislative and judiciary functions. Judges who are appointed Lords of Appeal become Barons and are entitled to a seat in the House of Lords for life. These judges are on their way from the House of Lords to Westminster Abbey, to celebrate the annual opening of the Law Courts in October.

RIGHT
HOUSES OF PARLIAMENT INTERIOR
Right in the heart of the Houses of Parliament is the Central Lobby, half way between the House of Commons and the House of Lords. This ornate octagonal hall, like most of the rest of the building, is handsomely decorated in the late-Gothic style, with statues of eminent statesmen standing on pedestals around the sides.

OVERLEAF
ST JAMES'S PARK AND BUCKINGHAM PALACE
The picturesque lake down the middle of this pretty park runs virtually all the way from the Queen Victoria Memorial, erected outside Buckingham Palace in 1811, to Downing Street, interrupted only by Duck Island, where numerous waterfowl breed in the spring.

LONDON'S HISTORY

Forty thousand years ago, when biologically modern human beings emerged in Europe, the climate in northern parts of the continent was extremely severe, and it is unlikely that many humans moved to the area where London now stands. By the end of the last ice age, around 10,000 BCE, Britain was still connected to Europe by land, and over the next few thousand years, in the Mesolithic and Neolithic periods, the ice melted, rivers and forests formed, and people began to settle in various areas along the Thames river. By 6500 BCE, the English Channel was formed by the melting of the ice sheets, people were forced out of the lower-lying valleys by flooding, and communities began to live in the upper woodlands along the banks of the west London Thames. The early Bronze Age, from 1800 BCE, was marked by increased wealth and comfort, when the Beaker people from central Europe dominated southeast Britain; but more climatic changes ousted this group and from 1400 BCE new centres, dominated by Celtic culture, emerged in the Thames valley. But by the last century BCE, the London region was little populated, and well outside the main areas of tribal intercourse and habitation.

When the Roman army, under the command of Aulus Plaudius, conquered Britain in CE 43, it quickly gained control of southeast England as far as the Thames, and the British tribes retreated into what is now the eastern county of Essex. The Emperor Claudius arrived to take command of the army, marched to Colchester, received the surrender of 11 British kings, and returned in triumph to Rome 16 days later. The Romans began to set up a military headquarters on the north side of the Thames, and within a few years had

constructed a bridge across the river, just a few yards to the east of the present London Bridge, and a town called Londinium at its northern end. Over the following 150 years, the Romans built a huge fort near Cripplegate, a basilica surrounded by a large forum, a palace for the governor, a defensive wall around the city and much else within. Londinium began to flourish as a trade centre and had a growing international population.

However, by the fifth century the Romans had gradually withdrawn and Britain was increasingly under the control of Anglo-Saxon invaders, who began to settle in small family and tribal groups around the country, largely ignoring towns like London except as bases for trade and transport across to Europe. Large parts of Lundenwic, as the town was then called, were in decline. Then came the Viking invasions in the eighth and ninth centuries, in which London was frequently stormed and its population slaughtered, before King Alfred of Wessex occupied it in 886, and he and his successors began its restoration and resettlement. More attacks from Scandinavia occurred toward the end of the tenth century, but London held out, and by the death of Edward the Confessor in 1066 the city had developed quite substantially, with many new houses and churches, and a new bridge replacing the lost Roman river crossing.

The Norman Conquest in 1066 signalled the real beginning of the London we know today. Westminster Abbey, started by Edward the Confessor, was completed in 1075. William I (William the Conqueror) began the building of the Tower of London in the 1080s. Construction of a new, stone-built London Bridge began in 1076 and was completed in 1209, lasting through many restorations

until 1832. By 1200 work had begun on the magnificent romanesque St Paul's Cathedral. This St Paul's survived until the Great Fire of 1666, after which the cathedral that stands today was designed and built at the end of the 17th century by Sir Christopher Wren on the same site. London's population grew rapidly, with perhaps as many as 80,000 people living within the old Roman walls. In the reigns of Henry III (1227–72) and Richard II (1377–99), Westminster began to develop as a separate town, dominated by the abbey and the royal palace next to it. As is still much the case today, the city was now Britain's capital and the centre of its trade, while the business of government was conducted at the monarch's base in Westminster.

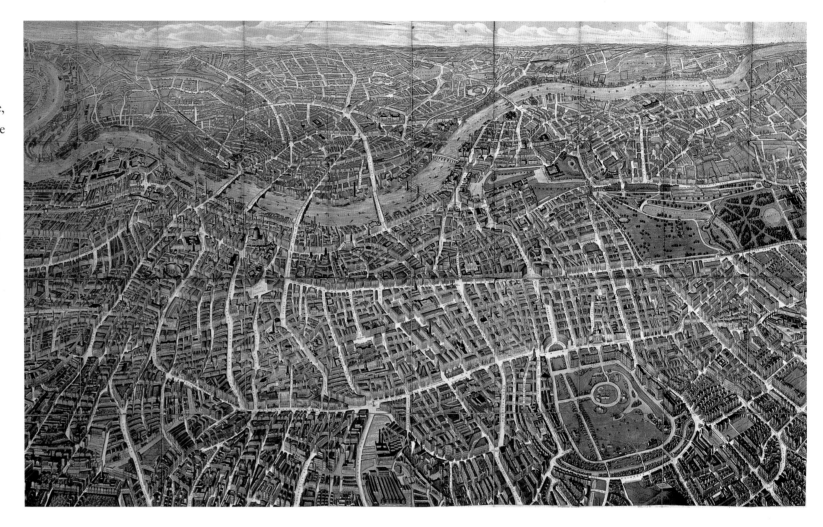

ABOVE
LONDON IN 1851
Six million people visited London during the Great Exhibition held in Hyde Park in 1851, and map-makers produced dozens of souvenir maps to provide for their needs. This balloon view, looking north from Southwark, was one of them, published by Banks & Co.

OPPOSITE
WESTMINSTER
This rendition of the Houses of Parliament is a stormy view painted by distinguished architect and artist John MacVicar Anderson (1835-1915) in the late 19th century. It hangs in the Museum of London in Aldersgate Street.

Commerce and trade increased rapidly in the 16th century, and London was now a flourishing port, trading with the continent of Europe. Still largely confined within the city walls, it was packed with cottages and houses, law courts, schools, almshouses, royal palaces and innumerable churches, and inhabited by rich and poor alike. Outside the wall to the north and east, in Shoreditch, Whitechapel and Shadwell, more buildings were erected to house the craftsmen and semi-skilled workers who serviced the growing trades, enlarging London's population threefold over the course of the century. Meanwhile rich and aristocratic Londoners tended to move west, around Holborn and down the Strand toward Westminster.

When the English Civil War broke out in the mid-17th century, a barrier of defences was built around London, which indicates how much larger the city had now become. They ran from Vauxhall to Wapping, north to Shoreditch, west to Hyde Park, and south down to Millbank. This was the city that was attacked by the Great Plague in 1665, which killed 70,000 citizens, and the Great Fire in 1666, which left the walled centre of London a blackened ruin, destroying some 13,300 houses, 52 company halls, 87 churches (including St Paul's Cathedral), and much else. Medieval London had been wiped out.

But the reconstruction, much of it funded by wealthy individuals who made their fortunes from trade and the acquisition of colonies around the world, was remarkable for both its speed and elegance, and by the middle of the 18th century London was transformed into one of the most stylish cities in Europe. By 1800, the population had risen to around a million, but despite the booming economy there was much poverty and

extreme overcrowding in the poorer areas, particularly in the East End. The rich continued to move west, along Piccadilly and Oxford Street. Among the best-known Georgian buildings still surviving from this period are the Bank of England and Mansion House in the City, the church of St Martin-in-the-Fields on Trafalgar Square, St Bartholomew's Hospital, Somerset House, and St George's, Hanover Square.

Through the long reign of Queen Victoria (1837-1901), London grew immensely, spreading out into the surrounding counties of Kent, Surrey, Middlesex, Hertfordshire and Essex. Huge areas of new housing went up, and the population rose to more than seven million people, many of them impoverished. The railways arrived in 1838, followed 25 years later by the first underground trains, with the more deeply tunnelled tubes coming in the 1880s. The City became the financial centre of the British Empire, with banks and insurance companies building their grand headquarters around the Bank of England. Whitehall, too, was transformed, housing the huge government offices required by the empire.

In the 20th century, despite severe ups and downs in the national economy, the City maintained its status as one of the world's leading financial centres. Many areas were destroyed in the bombing of World War II; and in the second half of the century the population began to decline (although it is now rising again). The port of London, on which the national economy had been dependent for so long, closed down in the 1960s, and has since been replaced with the hugely ambitious and largely successful development of London Docklands, now the centre of much of London's financial trade.

THE WHITE TOWER
This charming view of the medieval Tower of London, has Charles, Duke of Orléans, seated in the White Tower. It appears in his volume of collected poems, now housed in the British Library, and dates from around 1500.

THE GREAT FIRE
Dutch painter Lieve Pietersz Verschuier's view of the Great Fire of 1666 was probably painted on a visit to London shortly thereafter. Today it hangs in the Museum of Fine Arts in Budapest.

LINCOLN'S INN FIELDS
The largest square in central London, Lincoln's Inn
Fields was laid out in 1618 by Inigo Jones. This view,
painted by Samuel Scott (1702–72), belonging to the
Earl of Pembroke, hangs in Wilton House, Wiltshire.
Today most of the elegant 17th- and 18th-century
houses are lawyers' offices, but the fine Sir John
Soane's Museum is on the north side, and the Royal
College of Surgeons is located on the south side.

ST PAUL'S CATHEDRAL
The Italian painter Canaletto (1697-1768) lived and
worked in England for ten years from 1746, and
painted this magnificent work in 1754. It is now
part of the Paul Mellon Collection at the Yale
Center for British Art in New Haven, Connecticut.

OPPOSITE
TOWER BRIDGE IN WORLD WAR II
Charles Pears (1873–1958) was a distinguished marine artist, and during both World Wars was appointed an official war artist to the Admiralty. This work, painted in 1941, is entitled *The Pool of London during Dockland Air Raids*, and can be seen in the Guildhall Art Gallery in Aldermanbury.

ABOVE
VICTORY
The Prime Minister, Winston Churchill, joined the royal family at Buckingham Palace to celebrate the end of the World War II in 1945. From left to right: Princess Elizabeth (now Her Majesty The Queen), Queen Elizabeth, Churchill, King George VI and Princess Margaret.

THE THAMES

London's river is a much less busy highway than it was in earlier times, but it still provides a splendid insight into history. Many Londoners enjoy walking along the river banks, go rowing in Putney and Barnes, or take boats from Westminster Pier to Greenwich for an outing. Because it was for so many centuries a crucial element in the city's trade and industry, many stretches of the lower river remain harsh and ugly, and few of central London's grandest buildings face out over the river. But in recent decades this has begun to change, with developments such as the South Bank and the Isle of Dogs.

Taking a journey along the Thames in London, from its quiet stretches in the west of the city toward its estuary, east of the city, we start at Hampton Court, where Henry VIII acquired the palace in 1529, and the river is still gently flowing, unaffected by tidal forces. It runs past Thames Ditton Island, around Hampton Court Park, and through Kingston to Teddington, where the lock and weir mark the tidal dividing line. This is where the Port of London Authority, a public trust established in 1908, takes control of the Thames.

The river then swings past Eel Pie Island, where rock bands The Who and the Rolling Stones used to perform in the 1960s. The village of Ham is on the eastern side, and before long we encounter Ham House, an exceptionally attractive mansion built in 1610, one of the best survivals from this period in Europe, full of fine paintings and furniture, and believed to be haunted by the ghost of the Duchess of Lauderdale. On the other side is Marble Hill House, an equally magnificent Palladian villa which used to be the home of George II's mistress Henrietta Howard.

Apart from London Bridge, no Thames crossings were constructed until the 18th

century. Putney Bridge was built in 1729, and Richmond Bridge went up in 1777. These two bridges remain the oldest Thames crossings still in use in London. Beyond Richmond Bridge is the railway bridge and Twickenham Bridge, erected in 1933. Ahead is Isleworth Ait, a large island covered with poplars and willow trees, preserved by the Wildlife Trust and inhabited by treecreepers, kingfishers and herons. To the right is Old Deer Park, where stands the King's Observatory, built for George III in 1769, and where rugby, cricket and football are played. To the left is Syon House, owned by the earls and dukes of Northumberland since 1594, with its great stone lion which was moved here from Northumberland Avenue when their house there was demolished in 1873.

North of Old Deer Park is Kew Gardens, 300 acres containing a unique collection of trees and plants from all over the world, and now a UNESCO World Heritage Site. Across the river, beside the wharfs and docks of Old Brentford, is the Waterman's Art Centre, built in 1984 where an old gas works once stood.

Beyond Kew Bridge (the first version of which was built in 1758), and before the adjacent railway bridge, is Strand on the Green, with its attractive line of 18th-century houses facing southwest across the river. And beyond it is Chiswick Bridge. This is where the Oxford and Cambridge Boat Race ends, an event which has taken place virtually every year (except during war years) since 1845. The rowers come up-river from Putney, past the Wetland Centre in Barnes, under Hammersmith Bridge and round where the river swings south past the famous public school of St Paul's. Chiswick Mall, on the north side, is another fine row of 17th- and 18th-century houses, including Walpole

OPPOSITE

RICHMOND RIVERSIDE

The river frontage at Richmond upon Thames was redeveloped in 1988 to designs by the controversial architect Quinlan Terry (b. 1937), with more than twenty buildings in various classical styles, around four courtyards, and including shops, offices and a restaurant overlooking the river. Despite the objections of architectural critics, the area is highly popular with the local inhabitants. The elegant five-arched bridge beyond dates from 1777.

LEFT

HAMPTON COURT PALACE

The Great Gatehouse at the west front of Hampton Court Palace is one of the few parts that date back to the time of Cardinal Wolsey, Henry VIII's Lord Chancellor, who owned the palace from 1514 until 1528, when he fell from the King's favour. The moat bridge leading up to it, lined with elegant statues of the "King's Beasts", was added later by Henry. The King's extensions and enlargements of the palace were massive, costing about £18 million in today's money, and by the time it was finished in the 1540s Hampton Court Palace had become one of the grandest and most sophisticated palaces in England.

House, where Charles II's mistress, the Duchess of Cleveland, lived and died in 1709. Hammersmith Bridge is an impressive construction, designed by Sir Joseph Bazalgette and erected in 1887. In recent years it has periodically been closed, repaired and re-opened, and indeed was bombed by terrorists in June 2000.

Next comes Putney Bridge, the start of the Oxford and Cambridge Boat Race. Just to the north of it, hidden by the trees in its park along the river bank, is Fulham Palace, where the Bishops of London resided for almost 1,300 years until 1973. Ten of them are buried in All Saints Church beside the bridge. Beyond it is the Hurlingham Club, set in an attractive park where tennis, croquet, polo and cricket have been played since the middle of the 19th century. The river now moves north under Wandsworth Bridge, heading toward Chelsea. Many areas along both banks are currently being redeveloped, with housing, shopping and business centres.

The Chelsea stretch, from Battersea Bridge to Queenstown, includes the elegant Albert Bridge, designed by Roland Mason Ordish in 1873, and the attractive red-brick houses along Cheyne Walk and the Embankment. The grounds of the Royal Hospital, where the Chelsea Flower Show is held in May each year, stretch down to the river opposite Battersea Park. Beyond Chelsea Bridge is the huge, decaying Battersea Power Station, a listed building which over the next few years is planned to be redeveloped to include theatres, hotels, housing and offices.

Then the river turns north again toward Westminster, passing the striking headquarters of the Secret Intelligence Service (MI6) beside Vauxhall Bridge, and Tate Britain, the national collection of British art. The

domestic branch of the intelligence service, MI5, is further up, in the rather more dreary-looking Thames House on Millbank. Just beyond Lambeth Bridge is Lambeth Palace, where the Archbishops of Canterbury have lived for the last seven centuries.

As the river sweeps through Westminster the landscape is dominated by Big Ben and the Houses of Parliament, the former County Hall which contains the Saatchi Gallery, Dali Universe and London Aquarium, and the dominating but highly popular London Eye observation wheel. This is where the South Bank, one of London's crucial cultural centres, begins, dating from 1951 and dominated by the Royal Festival Hall. Across Hungerford Bridge on the north side is the striking new frontage of Charing Cross Station, and the Savoy Hotel facing onto Victoria Embankment.

Beyond Waterloo Bridge we begin to enter the oldest parts of London. The old Fleet River used to emerge into the Thames where Blackfriars Bridge stands, and beyond it is the new pedestrian Millennium Bridge leading across from Tate Modern to St Paul's Cathedral. Then there's Southwark Bridge, next to it Alexandra Railway Bridge, London Bridge, and finally Tower Bridge, with the view dominated by the Tower of London and the cruiser HMS Belfast, launched in 1938 and now a World War II naval museum.

But there is one more bridge to come. After the Thames swings round the Isle of Dogs, past Greenwich and the vast Millennium Dome, it widens past London City Airport and the Creekmouth and Thamesmead areas. By the time we get to the Queen Elizabeth II Bridge in Dartford, opened in October 1991 and Europe's largest cable-supported bridge, we are outside London and in the county of Kent.

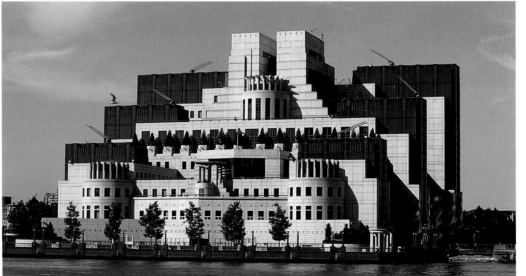

LAMBETH PALACE
The ancient London residence of the Archbishop of Canterbury is a modest red-brick building, and next to it is the church of St Mary Lambeth, now a museum devoted to the history of gardening. Lambeth Bridge, from which this view is taken, dates from 1936.

MI6
Terry Farrell's impressive building constructed for the Secret Intelligence Service in 1995 stands on the south bank of the river next to Vauxhall Bridge, and is more secure than it looks. In 2000 the Real IRA terrorist group assaulted it with an anti-tank missile, but caused little damage.

THE LONDON EYE

As part of the celebration of the millennium in 2000, a vast observation wheel 440ft high was erected on the Embankment next to County Hall, designed by the architects David Marks and Julia Barfield, and sponsored by British Airways and the Tussaud Group. Known as the London Eye, it was originally assumed to be no more than a temporary tourist attraction for the millennium year, and many Londoners disliked this huge object dominating almost every view in the West End. But over the last few years its popularity has increased greatly, and there is every reason to believe it has now become a permanent feature of the South Bank. The 32 spacious capsules take in about 25 people, and the wheel turns slowly round twice an hour, allowing some 15,000 visitors each day to enjoy a unique view across London. The most striking time to find yourself at the top of the London Eye is in the early evening, when the lights are going on around the city, but the sky is still bright enough to allow you to see as far as Hampstead in the north and Crystal Palace in the south.

HUNGERFORD BRIDGE
The view across the Thames from the South Bank
to Big Ben and the Houses of Parliament is
dominated by Hungerford railway bridge, built in
1864 with footbridges on either side. These have
recently been reconstructed with bright lights and
shiny pylons, to encourage pedestrians to walk
across the river to the South Bank.

TOWER BRIDGE
As Tower Bridge has become an internationally
recognized symbol of London, it surprises many
people to know that it is little more than 100 years
old, designed by Sir Horace Jones and opened in
1894. The bascules, raised here to allow boats
through, are lifted by hydraulic power. The bridge
contains an interesting museum, exhibiting evidence
of its history.

OPEN LATE FRIDAY & SATURDAY

MILLENNIUM BRIDGE
When Sir Norman Foster's footbridge was opened in 2000 it had to be closed immediately, because of the alarming vibrations that occurred when people began walking over it. These problems were solved a year later, and it is now an elegant and popular crossing between St Paul's Cathedral and Tate Modern.

THE THAMES BARRIER
In the 1950s and 1960s there were growing fears that tidal surges up the River Thames in the winter could flood many parts of London. This spectacular barrier located in Woolwich, with its nine reinforced concrete piers, was completed in 1984 and opened by the Queen the following year.

THE DOME
The Millennium Dome was built in 1999 to house an exhibition offering a portrait of Britain at the turn of the millennium. It is situated on the Greenwich peninsula, which formerly contained a huge gasworks and was polluted with industrial chemicals; so the Dome's construction brought at least one major benefit to the area. However, the huge building remains an unsolved problem, now closed and unused. The latest scheme proposed is to open it as a technology business park.

GREENWICH

The strikingly beautiful Royal Naval College, today occupied by the University of Greenwich, has a centuries-old history. It stands on what was once the site of Henry VIII's favourite Palace of Placentia, where he married two of his six wives, Catherine of Aragon and Anne of Cleves. In the 17th century the palace was demolished, and eventually replaced by the Greenwich Hospital, mainly designed by Sir Christopher Wren. The hospital was taken over by the Royal Naval College in 1763. A few hundred yards to the west is Greenwich Pier, one of the region's main attractions. Here the elegant Cutty Sark, a sailing clipper built in 1869 to carry tea from China to England, now rests in its own dry dock, where it is visited by hundreds of thousands of tourists every year. Nearby is Gipsy Moth IV, the yacht in which Sir Francis Chichester circumnavigated the world single-handed in 1966–67.

GREENWICH

The strikingly beautiful Royal Naval College, today occupied by the University of Greenwich, has a centuries-old history. It stands on what was once the site of Henry VIII's favourite Palace of Placentia, where he married two of his six wives, Catherine of Aragon and Anne of Cleves. In the 17th century the palace was demolished, and eventually replaced by the Greenwich Hospital, mainly designed by Sir Christopher Wren. The hospital was taken over by the Royal Naval College in 1763. A few hundred yards to the west is Greenwich Pier, one of the region's main attractions. Here the elegant Cutty Sark, a sailing clipper built in 1869 to carry tea from China to England, now rests in its own dry dock, where it is visited by hundreds of thousands of tourists every year. Nearby is Gipsy Moth IV, the yacht in which Sir Francis Chichester circumnavigated the world single-handed in 1966–67.

ROYAL LONDON

Although London was inhabited from time to time by Anglo-Saxon kings before the Norman Conquest, including Alfred the Great (849-99) and Harold I (d.1040), its royal history really begins when King Edward the Confessor embarked on the rebuilding of Westminster Abbey in 1050, on the site of the old monastery of St Peter, and built a palace nearby so he could oversee it. Edward was too ill to attend the Abbey's consecration in December 1065, dying the following month, and his successor Harold II had no time to move into the new palace before being killed at the Battle of Hastings in October 1066. The French conqueror, William I, was crowned king of England on 25 December that year, and in 1078 he began the construction of the Tower of London, completing the White Tower by 1088. But Westminster Palace, to which Westminster Hall was added in 1097, remained his and his successors' principal residence for the following four centuries.

A royal residence existed in the small fishing village of Greenwich in the 13th century, although over the following 200 years it was granted to various kinsmen. Henry VIII was born there in 1491, and his first marriage, to Catherine of Aragon, took place there in 1509 – although he later spent more time in Bridewell or his new Nonsuch Palace in Sutton, until he acquired Hampton Court from Cardinal Wolsey in 1525. Monarchs Elizabeth I, James I and Charles I all resided in Greenwich. In 1616 Inigo Jones began the building of the Queen's House, which still dominates the Royal Naval College, itself now part of the University of Greenwich.

Hampton Court Palace meanwhile was further enlarged by Henry VIII, and in the mid-17th century Charles II added further

rooms at the southeast corner of the palace, to house his mistress Lady Castlemaine. But the biggest changes came at the end of the 17th century, in the reign of William and Mary, when the king's and queen's main apartments were rebuilt, designed by Sir Christopher Wren, on the site of the old Tudor apartments. Finally, the Cumberland Suite, designed by William Kent, was added in 1732. Today the palace and its beautiful grounds are permanently open to the public.

By the beginning of the 16th century, because Westminster Palace had become dominated by the royal court in all its aspects – judicial, administrative and parliamentary – Henry VIII began the construction of two new palaces in Westminster. The first was Cardinal Wolsey's York House, transformed into Whitehall Palace in 1515, but destroyed by fire in 1698. Its superb Banqueting House, built by Inigo Jones in 1619-22, is its only surviving element. Second, in 1531, on the site of the medieval leper hospital of St James, Henry VIII began the construction of St James's Palace, which was completed by 1540. It is still occupied by members of the present royal family – the Princess Royal, and Princess Alexandra – and is still officially the residence of the sovereign, which is why foreign ambassadors are formally accredited to "the Court of St James's". York House next to it belongs to the Duke of Kent. Services are held every Sunday in the Chapel Royal, which the public can attend. The Queen's Chapel, designed by Inigo Jones in 1623, stands on the other side of Marlborough Road.

When William and Mary came to the throne in 1689, their preference was for Kensington Palace, which they acquired from the Earl of Nottingham and enlarged under the designs of Sir Christopher Wren. Queen

OPPOSITE
THE GOLDEN JUBILEE
The Queen's dazzling Gold State Coach was designed for George III by William Chambers in the 18th century, and is normally reserved for coronation ceremonies. It was used most recently in June 2002, when the Queen and the Duke of Edinburgh travelled to St Paul's Cathedral as part of the four-day Golden Jubilee celebrations to commemorate 50 years of her reign.

LEFT
ROYAL SENTRIES
Two members of the Queen's Household Guards, in their distinctive red tunics and bearskin hats, prepare to exchange positions on duty in a sentry box outside Buckingham Palace.

Victoria was born here in 1819. Royal family members also still live in this elegant building on the western edge of Kensington Gardens, and when Diana, Princess of Wales died in 1997 this is where the vast crowds of mourners came to leave their huge piles of flowers.

Clarence House, on the Mall beside St James's Palace, was the home of Elizabeth, the widow of George VI, for almost half a century until she died in 2002. Built in 1825 by John Nash, it is now the official London residence of the Prince of Wales. Lancaster House, adjacent to it, is an imposing mansion built by Benjamin Wyatt in 1825-27 for the Duke of York, and is now a Government conference centre. The ground-floor rooms of Clarence House can be visited by the general public in the summer on a guided tour. They still contain much of the works of art and furniture belonging to Elizabeth, who, in widowhood, became known as Queen Elizabeth, The Queen Mother.

Buckingham Palace, the Queen's official London residence, was built in 1703 as the town house of the Duke of Buckingham, and purchased by George III in 1761. All but one of George III's 14 children were born there. His heir, George IV, decided to transform it into a palace, and employed the renowned architect John Nash to design suitable enlargements and embellishments, at vast expense to the public. Nash was eventually sacked for over-spending, and after George IV's death in 1830 Edward Blore took over the completion of the work. The palace was eventually finished six years later, and the first monarch to reside there was Queen Victoria, who moved in three weeks after her accession in 1837. She, too, made further changes, enclosing the forecourt between the projecting wings. The front of the palace was remodelled in the reign of her grandson George V in 1913, when the Victoria Memorial was erected outside the gates in the Mall. In addition to its grand state rooms and offices, the Palace also includes the Queen's Gallery, open daily to show splendid exhibitions of the royal collection of works of art and artifacts; and the Royal Mews, with a fine display of royal carriages and state coaches.

Every summer during July and August members of the public are given access to the state rooms, but in limited numbers lead by tour leaders. Also in July the Queen gives a series of garden parties, inviting around 8,000 guests to each occasion. A wide range of British and Commonwealth citizens from all walks of life are invited, and the parties take place on the expansive green lawns of the extensive Palace garden.

If you want to know whether the Queen is currently residing at her London home, look to see if the royal standard flag is flying above the central arch.

RIGHT AND OPPOSITE
WESTMINSTER ABBEY
Edward the Confessor (c.1003–1066) constructed Westminster Abbey on the site of a Benedictine abbey, consecrating it in 1065, and he and virtually all his successors until George III (1738–1820) are buried there. This, too, is where all of the English monarchs, except Edward V and Edward VIII, have been crowned. The Abbey remains one of the most beautiful surviving examples of the Early English architectural style, and contains some equally stunning later additions, such as Henry VII's perpendicular chapel at the east end, and the towers designed by Nicholas Hawksmoor in 1739. Among its best-known areas are Poets' Corner in the south transept, and the Tomb of the Unknown Warrior at the west entrance.

BUCKINGHAM PALACE STATE DINING ROOM
In the royal palaces around the country, such as
Windsor, Sandringham and Balmoral, there is no
shortage of space for dining and entertainment.
But the grandest space is the state dining room in
Buckingham Palace, designed by John Nash in 1825,
with its heavily carved ceiling, and royal portraits
hanging on the red damask-clad walls. The table
can comfortably seat 46 people around it.

OVERLEAF, FOLDOUT
BUCKINGHAM PALACE
The Queen's London residence, originally called
into its grand state in the 1820s to designs by
John Nash. The east front, seen here, was added
by Queen Victoria in 1847.

LEFT
ST JAMES'S PALACE
The gatehouse of St James's Palace, facing up
St James's Street toward Piccadilly, is one of the
oldest surviving parts of this picturesque brick
building, originally constructed by Henry VIII in
the 1530s on the site of a leper hospital

RIGHT
KENSINGTON PALACE
Formally Kensington Court, this attractive red brick
building was originally a grand mansion owned by
the earls of Nottingham, until William III bought it
in 1689 and enlarged it under the designs of Sir
Christopher Wren. Queen Victoria was born here,
and toward the end of the 20th century it was
famously the residence of Diana, Princess of Wales.

FAR RIGHT
THE ROYAL NAVAL COLLEGE, GREENWICH
Henry VIII's Palace of Placentia was demolished
around 1700 and replaced with Christopher Wren's
Greenwich Hospital, which became the Royal Naval
College, shown here with its twin domes. But at
the back it still contains the beautiful Queen's
House, built for James I's wife Anne, designed by
Inigo Jones and completed in 1635.

OPPOSITE
TROOPING THE COLOUR

Every year in June the Queen's official birthday is celebrated by a ceremonial event in Horse Guard's Parade called Trooping the Colour, in which one of the regiments in the British Army's Household Division – the Blues and Royals, Life Guards, Grenadier, Coldstream, Scots, Irish and Welsh Guards – parades in her honour, with a huge audience of the general public watching from the side-seats. For many years the Queen used to appear at this event on horseback, but since 1986 she sits in a Victorian phaeton.

TOP LEFT
COLDSTREAM GUARDS

One of the Queen's regiments, the Coldstream Guards regularly participate in royal ceremonies, dressed in their elegant 18th-century uniforms. They can be identified by the red plumes on the right-hand side of their bearskin helmets.

TOP RIGHT
PRINCES

Other members of the royal household also attend annual ceremonial events, riding on horseback or by royal coach along the Mall to Horse Guards. Here, the Queen's son Prince Andrew, the Duke of York, is seen with his two nephews, princes William and Harry, the sons of the late Princess Diana.

LEFT
THE BAND OF THE IRISH GUARDS

Each regiment of the Household Division has a regimental band, all of which have well-deserved reputations for musical excellence. Here, the Irish Guards' band is seen marching down The Mall, led by the regiment's mascot, an Irish wolfhound.

HAMPTON COURT PALACE

This palace is a fascinating amalgam of architectural styles and features, from the Tudor west entrance (left), which includes the mounted lion statues (above) complete with their royal shields, to the Wren-designed state apartments at the eastern end (opposite). George II was the last monarch to reside at Hampton Court, in the mid-18th century, and the palace was opened to the public by Queen Victoria in 1838. It contains a wealth of fine works of art from the royal collections, including some magnificent tapestries from the Tudor period, and paintings collected by Charles I by artists such as Bronzino, Corregio, Van Dyke and Rubens.

THE KING'S APARTMENTS
Built for William and Mary at the very end of the 17th century, these magnificent state apartments overlook the equally stunning, formal Privy Garden at Hampton Court Palace. The garden has recently been carefully restored to how it would have looked when first created in 1702.

THE GREAT PARKS

Although Greater London is mostly a huge and densely populated urban metropolis, it contains a surprisingly large range of peaceful open spaces, covering around 70 square miles. There are historic royal parks, municipal parks created in the last two centuries, ancient common lands, squares containing public gardens, and old cemeteries and churchyards – as well as numerous sports fields, reservoirs, abandoned former built-up areas and railway embankments. An interesting range of wildlife and rare plants exists within the city, including an influx over recent decades of foxes, birds of prey, and grass snakes.

Dominating the centre of London are Kensington Gardens, Hyde Park, Green Park and St James's Park, and these great open spaces make it possible to walk almost non-stop across green land for nearly three miles, from Black Lion Gate on Bayswater Road to Great George Street in Westminster.

Hyde Park covers 350 acres, and was appropriated from the monks of Westminster Cathedral by Henry VIII in 1536. Henry turned it into one of his deer parks for hunting and other private activities. It was opened to the public at the beginning of the 17th century in the reign of James I. Kensington Gardens was originally attached to Kensington Palace, and was added to Hyde Park by William IV in the early 19th century, making the combined area of the two spaces more than 600 acres. Among its varied attractions Hyde Park boasts the Serpentine Gallery, founded in 1970 on a site where a tea pavilion was erected in 1934; rowing on the Serpentine lake; Speaker's Corner beside Marble Arch, where orators hold forth on their varied subjects every Sunday, following a tradition begun in the mid-19th century; the

Albert Memorial at the southern end, opposite the Royal Albert Hall; the Peter Pan statue at the northern end of the Long Water; and the Lido on the south side of the Serpentine, where Londoners sunbathe and swim in warm weather. At the Round Pond innumerable model yachts and boats are sailed at weekends, mainly by members of the Model Yacht Sailing Association, founded in 1876. Nearby is the new Princess Diana Memorial Fountain, opened in July 2004.

Green Park is a pleasant, tree-lined, 40-acre space, located between Picadilly and the Mall, but is surprisingly short of buildings and artifacts – apart from a bandstand half-way down Queen's Walk. St James's Park is much more striking, with its birdkeeper's cottage, lavish flowerbeds, the romantic lake designed by the renowned Regency architect John Nash (1752–1835), and the surrounding palaces and government buildings.

By far the most ambitious project undertaken by John Nash, included the development of Regent's Park. Soon after the Prince Regent assumed power in 1811, Nash won a competition for plans to develop the Marylebone Park estate, including connecting the park to the Prince's residence in Carlton House. Thus he created Oxford Circus, Regent Street and Waterloo Place, the largest and most striking street development in London's history. Around the park are his spectacular terraces, decorated with pediments and statues, and several villas within. The Park today is full of lively activities and attractions, including the London Zoo at the northern end, the Open

GREEN PARK
Thousands of daffodils carpet the eastern side of this central London park each year in the spring.

Air Theatre in Queen Mary's Gardens, rowing on the huge Boating Lake, children's playgrounds, tennis centres, a golf school, running tracks and sports grounds. Regent's College, by the Inner Circle, houses several academic institutions, including the School of Psychotherapy and the European Business School. At the western side is the London Central Mosque, presented as a gift to the Muslim community by the government in 1944, designed by Frederick Gibberd, and completed in 1978. Nearby, on the other side of Outer Circle, is Winfield House, built for the Woolworth heiress Barbara Hutton in 1936, and now the residence of the US ambassador. On the eastern side of the park, where most of Nash's terraces stand, is the elegant Georgian St Katharine's, the church of the Danish community in London. Threading along the northern end is Regent's Canal, which runs from Paddington to Hackney. When this was built in 1820 it was seen as a vital commercial facility for transporting goods, but the arrival of the railways a few years later made it obsolete. The London Canal Museum near King's Cross Station tells its history.

A far wilder London park is Hampstead Heath, 825 acres of grass and woodland just to the north of central London, with the grounds of Kenwood House (which contains the Iveagh Bequest art collection) on its northern side, and Parliament Hill (with its fine view of London) to the south. The pub called Jack Straw's Castle, on the road crossing at the Vale of Health, dates back to the 14th century; and Spaniards Inn, along Spaniards Road, has been there since 1630. There are three open-air swimming pools on the Heath: Kenwood Pond for women only, Highgate Pond for men, and Hampstead Pond for both.

Holland Park, half a mile west of Kensington Gardens, was the garden of Holland House; a Jacobean mansion until it was largely destroyed by wartime bombing in 1941. The derelict estate was acquired by London County Council in 1952, parts of the house restored, and the beautiful wooded gardens opened to the public. Opera and ballet are performed in the Open Air Theatre here in the summer, and there is a fine restaurant, a popular outdoor cafe, and two art galleries also in the park.

Among the less central green areas is the splendid 200-acre Victoria Park, in south Hackney to the east of central London, and Battersea Park, which was laid out in 1853, and contains a boating lake, a children's zoo, and the Japanese Peace Pagoda facing out over the Thames. Much the largest park in London is Richmond Park in the southwest. Its 2,500 acres were a royal hunting ground in the Middle Ages, and became enclosed in 1637 by Charles I. Several hundred red and fallow deer still roam around the ancient oak woods. Not far away, on the other side of Kingston Bridge, is Bushy Park, next to the magnificent Hampton Court Park.

The Royal Botanic Gardens at Kew began in the 1730s, when the son of George II, Prince Frederick, and his wife Princess Augusta, were living in Kew Farm, close to Richmond Lodge where his parents lived.

RIGHT
REGENT'S PARK
A grand building on the western side of the park, built by Regency architect John Nash.

OPPOSITE
KENSINGTON GARDENS
The Round Pond, situated on the western side of the park next to Kensington Palace, is highly popular with both local Londoners keen on model-boat sailing, and a large number of geese.

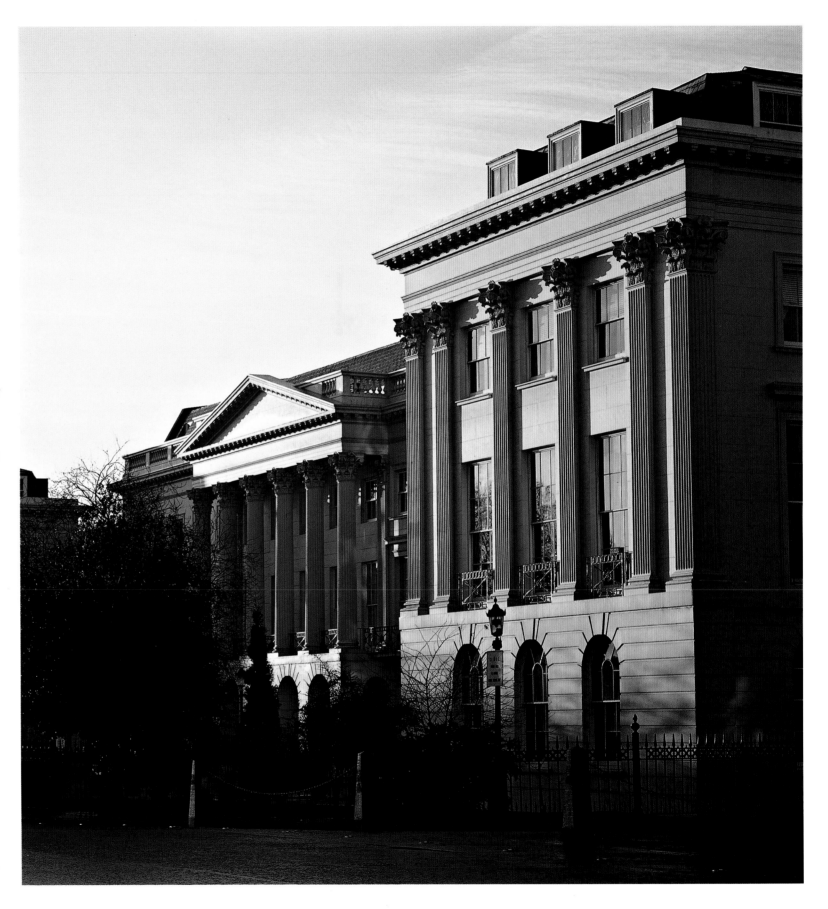

They were both passionate about gardening, expanded the estate and planted a huge range of trees in the landscaped gardens. After Frederick's death in 1751, much lamented by the English gardening fraternity, Augusta continued to maintain the gardens, helped by her friend the Earl of Bute, who had a keen desire to create a garden that would "contain all the plants known on earth". The 300 acres at Kew are recognized today as home to one of the world's leading botanic gardens, with magnificent glass-houses and a collection of more than 30,000 different plants, and were accorded UNESCO World Heritage Site status in 2003.

Another historic park is Greenwich, behind the National Maritime Museum and stretching up the hill past the Old Royal Observatory. This spot always provided a stunning view of the Thames and London, and still does today. Beyond it is Blackheath, where Wat Tyler assembled his troops in the Peasants' Revolt in 1381, and where the annual London Marathon begins.

London contains many other parks, large and small. Wormwood Scrubs, northwest of White City, is famous for its prison but also contains a local nature reserve. Archbishop's Park, near Lambeth Palace, is smaller and much less well known, but equally pleasant with its tennis courts and cricket pitches. And Primrose Hill, just north of Regent's Park, offers a stunning view over central London.

ABOVE AND RGHT
THE ALBERT MEMORIAL
This splendid Gothic monument to Queen Victoria's consort Prince Albert, at the southern side of Hyde Park, was designed by Sir George Gilbert Scott and opened to the public in 1872. This almost excessively imposing sculpture was largely funded by the profits from the 1851 Great Exhibition, which Prince Albert himself had conceived and masterminded. The memorial has recently undergone full restoration, which included regilding the impressive statue of Albert – the original gilding had been removed in World War I.

RIGHT, TOP
PRIMROSE HILL
North of Regent's Park and London Zoo is Primrose Hill, rising 210 feet above sea level, and providing a striking view of the city.

BELOW
WESTMINSTER SCHOOL
Behind Westminster Abbey is the distinguished Westminster School, dating back to the 14th century and refounded by Elizabeth I in 1560. Here in Abbey Garden, part of the school, a brass band performs for visitors.

RIGHT, BOTTOM
THE ORANGERY AT KENSINGTON PALACE
Kensington Palace is a royal residence, but the beautiful Orangery, built by Hawksmoor and Vanbrugh in 1704, is open to the public, serving traditional English afternoon tea.

LEFT

PETER PAN

George Frampton's bronze statue of Peter Pan in Kensington Gardens, sculpted in 1912, attracts many young visitors. Peter Pan's creator J.M. Barrie used to live nearby, on the northern edge of the park.

BELOW

HYDE PARK

A number of state and private schools are located around the edges of Hyde Park, and their urban pupils, some of whom are seen here taking a stroll in their school uniforms, benefit greatly from the park's huge open spaces.

KEW GARDENS
The grandest of Kew's seven glasshouses is the Palm House, next to the pond on the eastern side, designed by Decimus Burton and completed in 1848. It is probably the world's most important surviving Victorian glass-and-iron structure.

OPPOSITE
RICHMOND PARK DEER
One unique feature of Richmond Park is its mass of several hundred red and fallow deer, which roam freely throughout its 2,500 acres.

VILLAGE LONDON

Although London expanded so massively in the 19th century, sprawling out into the surrounding counties, and at one time becoming the largest metropolis in the world, it is an inescapable fact that many of its parts retain their individual village character, with their own high streets, ancient parish churches, village greens and town halls. Their histories vary greatly, largely depending on the era when they became absorbed into the city, and some are more recognizable than others. But Londoners generally feel their home is their village, rather than the borough of which it is a part, let alone the city as a whole.

Chelsea is an obvious example, with a long riverside history from at least Saxon times. Sir Thomas More lived in Beaufort House, and Henry VIII built a manor house in what is now Cheyne Walk, occupied later by the physician Sir Hans Sloane (1660-1753), whose library of 50,000 volumes became the nucleus of the British Museum. At the heart of Chelsea lies the King's Road, leading into Sloane Square, which is dominated by the Peter Jones department store at one end and the Royal Court Theatre at the other.

Stoke Newington, in north London, is at least as ancient, and contains some beautiful 17th-century houses in Newington Green. Hampstead, too, dates back to Saxon times but, with its adjacent Heath, today has a more rural atmosphere than Stoke Newington.

Hampstead Garden Suburb, in the north of London, was created from scratch in 1907 by a local heiress, Dame Henrietta Barnett, who purchased 20 acres of land and employed the architect Sir Edwin Lutyens to design the Central Square. Another, slightly earlier, example of a London village designed and built in this way is Bedford Park in Acton, west London, initiated by cloth merchant

Jonathan Carr. In 1875 he bought 24 acres near Turnham Green, and employed E.W. Godwin as his initial architect; but the most striking houses were designed by Norman Shaw.

Putney, Mortlake and Barnes each have their own village atmosphere, particularly the latter with its attractive green and duck-pond, and its medieval church of St Mary's. Rumour has it that the Barnes air is so healthy that more twins are born there than anywhere else in London. Blackheath, south of Greenwich, was developed specifically as a village in the mid-19th century, and nestles in a dip below the open, treeless heath. It has a pleasant range of pubs and restaurants, and a splendid Victorian concert hall in Lee Road. Dulwich, on the other hand, has been a village since at least the tenth century. The land was bought by the actor-manager Edward Alleyn in 1605, and he founded the school Dulwich College 14 years later. The almshouses that were part of his foundation are still in use; and a few yards away is the Dulwich Picture Gallery, designed by Sir John Soane and opened in 1817, with its fine collection of old masters.

The village of Wandsworth has a long history too, and in the 16th century became an established haven for immigrants. The French Huguenot refugees in the 18th century created a thriving industrial area, and their crafts and market gardens made the area famous. Huge areas of housing were built in the 19th century, and vast council blocks in the 1950s after World War II damage. But Wandsworth still retains a strong local

OPPOSITE
LITTLE VENICE
Along the Regent's Canal by Warwick Avenue is a tranquil green oasis, named Little Venice by poet Robert Browning, where numerous house boats and narrow barges line the canal. Neighbouring Maida Vale is a typical London village.

atmosphere, with its own town hall and a busy shopping centre on the High Street. Most of the housing around Wandsworth Common has been gentrified in the last few decades.

Now part of west London, Ealing was a small rural village in the 18th century. When the railways and trams arrived in the 19th century, Ealing quickly became a large suburban residential area, with industrial estates in the outer parts. But surprising elements of old Ealing survive, such as coaching inns like the Original Old Hatte and the Green Man in the Broadway, the 18th-century Pitshanger Manor (now a museum), and Georgian cottages on Ealing Green. This is the location of Ealing Studios, currently being redeveloped, where many famous comedy films were made in the 1950s and '60s.

Ealing's neighbour Acton also has a long history. Acton is mentioned in the Domesday Book of 1086, and its church of St Mary's dates from at least the 13th century. It was briefly fashionable in Stuart times as a spa, when mineral-bearing springs were found at

Acton Wells; and like Ealing it grew rapidly in the 19th century as an industrial and residential centre. Acton's large Victorian town hall is at present being restored and developed into a library, market and conference centre.

Not all London villages have long roots in the past, or were specially created in the 19th and 20th centuries by millionaires. For example, Notting Hill was a Victorian urban development, and in the 1950s a notorious slum. But gentrification over the last half century – and perhaps the influence of the film *Notting Hill* – have turned it into one of London's most desirable areas. The same is true of places such as Pimlico, Maida Vale, Battersea and Clapham.

For the truly rich there is no more elegant London village than Mayfair, developed from the 1720s between Regent Street and Park Lane. During the 20th century, many of its grand mansions were destroyed by bombing or converted into flats and offices, but in recent years this process has reversed and the residential population has begun to grow again.

OPPOSITE
THE ROYAL HOSPITAL
Along Chelsea Embankment is Christopher Wren's magnificent Royal Hospital, built in 1682–92, and the home of 400 elderly soldiers known as Chelsea pensioners. The pensioners can often be seen in the local area wearing their distinctive scarlet coats.

FAR LEFT
WOLFGANG AMADEUS MOZART
Off Lower Sloane Street is a statue of Mozart, erected in honour of the eight-year-old composer's 15-month visit to London in 1763–4. For a time he lived at 180 Ebury Street, where he composed his first symphony.

LEFT
A CHELSEA PENSIONER
The Royal Hospital still provides a comfortable and caring environment, with excellent medical facilities, for elderly and disabled soldiers. To be eligible to join you must be a male army pensioner, at least 55 years old, with no wife or family to support.

BEDFORD PARK
On the boundary between Chiswick and Acton is the pleasant Victorian Bedford Park with its elegant red-brick houses, many designed by Norman Shaw in the Queen Anne style.

FOURNIER STREET, SPITALFIELDS
Running between Old Spitalfields Market and Brick Lane, this street contains an almost unbroken line of fine Georgian houses built in the 1720s by Samuel Worrell, topped with lofts for silk-weavers. In 2004 they were selling for around £1.5 million each.

LEFT
TITE STREET
Crossing Royal Hospital Road in Chelsea, Tite Street has been the residence of many famous people over the last 150 years, including Oscar Wilde, Mark Twain, James Whistler and John Singer Sargent.

BELOW
9 NORTHUMBERLAND PLACE
In the 1960s most of Notting Hill was a famous slum, but 40 years later there was a political scandal concerning the Labour politician Peter Mandelson's acquisition of this modest late-19th-century house.

OVERLEAF LEFT
QUEEN'S GATE
Running all the way down from Kensington Gardens to Old Brompton Road, this wide, grand road provides the western border to London University's Imperial College and the vast elegant building that houses the Natural History Museum.

OVERLEAF RIGHT
PALACE GARDEN TERRACE, KENSINGTON
Although it runs straight up to Notting Hill Gate, and contains the Arc Restaurant at number 122, this is a quiet street lined with cherry trees. The houses are larger than they seem, and currently sell for more than £3 million apiece.

LONDON PILLARBOX
Like the traditional red telephone boxes, London's red post boxes, also called pillarboxes, are highly visible features in many streets. They were first introduced in 1879, and each displays the times of post collection on the front.

SHEPHERD MARKET
Tucked between Piccadilly and Curzon Street in the heart of Mayfair, Shepherd Market is a charming, affluent village-like area of small shops, and bars and restaurants, and contains one of London's finest pubs, Ye Grapes, which was built in 1882.

STRAND-ON-THE-GREEN
Situated along the northern bank of the River
Thames east of Kew Bridge, this is a surprisingly
peaceful and secluded stretch of fine riverside
houses. The City Barge pub, shown here, has a
charter dating back to the 15th century.

83

NOTTING HILL CARNIVAL

Every year since 1966, on the last weekend in August, Notting Hill has hosted the Notting Hill Carnival. Inspired by the immigration of many Caribbean peoples to this area after 1948, Carnival was, in the early years, a modest local summer celebration. However, in the last few decades it has attracted as many as two million visitors from all over London, as well as many tourists, to what is now seen as a major multicultural arts festival. Today, as well as the traditional Trinidadian music and dancing, groups participate from Afghanistan, Kurdistan, Bangladesh, the Philippines, Bulgaria, Brazil and many other places, representing the range of cultures and ethnicities for which London is now famous. Some claim it is the second-greatest carnival in the world, after that of Rio de Janeiro.

STRAND-ON-THE-GREEN
Situated along the northern bank of the River Thames east of Kew Bridge, this is a surprisingly peaceful and secluded stretch of fine riverside houses. The City Barge pub, shown here, has a charter dating back to the 15th century.

THE CITY

The ancient City of London covers no more than one square mile, from Temple Bar in the Strand to Aldgate in the east, and from the river up to Finsbury Square and Barbican. This small but tightly built area has its own borough council (the Corporation of London), and its own police force; and for two centuries it has been, and remains, one of the most important commercial and financial centres in the world.

In its long history, the City has been densely populated, with as many as a million inhabitants by the end of the 18th century, many of them immigrants from elsewhere in Britain and Europe. But over the succeeding two centuries the population declined dramatically, and today only a few thousand people actually live there, augmented every weekday by the 300,000 people who work in the mainly financial and legal professions within the square mile.

The western side of the City has for several centuries been dominated by lawyers and journalists. Until 1987 virtually all Britain's national newspapers were located in and around Fleet Street (today many of them are in the newly developed Docklands). The vast Royal Courts of Justice building, erected in 1872, is located in the Strand just outside the City boundary, and around it are the ancient Inns of Court – the Middle Temple and Inner Temple on either side of Middle Temple Lane, Lincoln's Inn in Holborn and Gray's Inn to the north – which house the offices of leading solicitors and barristers. The Central Criminal Court, better known as the Old Bailey, is on the corner of Newgate Street. Despite severe bomb damage during World War II there are still some fine old buildings in these areas, including the 12th-century Temple Church, and the ravishing

Middle Temple hall in Fountain Court, completed in 1573. Fetter Lane, running north from Fleet Street up to High Holborn, is where the Great Fire in 1666 finally stopped, and for many centuries it has been a symbol of the city's border.

Heading east down Fleet Street to Ludgate Circus, we approach the subterranean course of the River Fleet, which from ancient times was the City's western boundary, emerging into the Thames by Blackfriars Bridge. It became foully polluted over the centuries, and was eventually covered over in 1765. Ahead, up Ludgate Hill, is Sir Christopher Wren's great masterpiece St Paul's Cathedral, on a site where three previous cathedrals have stood since 604CE.

Queen Victoria Street now leads directly to the heart of the City, where the great financial institutions have been based for centuries. The Bank of England and the Stock Exchange still

OPPOSITE
ST PAUL'S CATHEDRAL INTERIOR
When its medieval predecessor burned down in the Great Fire of 1666, Sir Christopher Wren designed this architectural masterpiece in the Renaissance style, with beautifully carved Portland stonework, completed by 1710. The fine nave leads up to the great space beneath the magnificent dome, with spandrels of mosaic designed by the Venetian artist Salviati. Energetic visitors can climb 530 stairs to the top of the dome, and enjoy stunning views both of the cathedral's interior and, outside, the City of London and beyond.

ABOVE, LEFT
ENTRANCE TO THE CITY
The City of London's coat of arms, dating back at least to the 17th century, consists of a central flag of St George with St Paul's sword in the left-hand side, enclosed between a pair of dragons, with the Latin motto Domine dirige nos ("Lord direct us"). Statues of these dramatic dragons are dotted around the boundaries of the City, in Temple Bar, Shoreditch and elsewhere.

ABOVE
THE ROYAL EXCHANGE
Dominating the corner between Threadneedle Street and Cornhill, the impressive Royal Exchange building was designed by Sir William Tite in 1844, and in the 1980s housed the London International Financial Futures Exchange (LIFFE), now in Cannon Street. The inner courtyard contains a popular eating place, the Grand Café and Bar.

dominate this small area, along with Mansion House and the Royal Exchange Building, and the offices of great merchant banks, clearing banks, insurance companies and building societies. Of the 500 largest companies in the world, 375 have offices the City. The dominating skyscrapers include Lord Foster's recently completed headquarters for Swiss Re in St Mary Axe, known to all as the "gherkin", Richard Seifert's Tower 42 in Old Broad Street, and the Lloyd's of London building at 1 Lime Street designed by Richard Rogers.

A vivid echo of the City's past can be found among the narrow and winding streets: more than 50 old churches, many of them designed by Wren. They have survived the centuries, including the Blitz and more recent terrorist attacks, but are little used today because the City has so few inhabitants. But many of them are worth exploring, such as St Andrew by the Wardrobe in Queen Victoria Street, St Mary Woolnoth in Lombard Street, and St Giles Cripplegate, where Oliver Cromwell was married and John Milton is buried. There are also nearly a hundred city livery companies, some of them dating back as far as the 12th century, and many still housed in elegant buildings within the square mile. Many of their fine halls – such as Goldsmiths' Hall in Foster Lane or Merchant Taylors' Hall in Threadneedle Street – can be rented by the public for receptions and dinner parties.

If we head down King William Street toward the river, we approach the Monument, erected by Parliament in memory of the Great Fire, which broke out in a bakery in nearby Pudding Lane in September 1666. Beyond it is London Bridge, and Old Billingsgate, which was once a famous fish market, now found further down river by Canary Wharf. Beside Old Billingsgate is the rather elegant, early-

19th-century Custom House. A few yards downriver is the Tower of London, the captial's most admired tourist attraction. The central White Tower was constructed in the 1070s, and further extensions, new towers, the wall and the moat were added over the following 200 years. Because this historic building has been carefully restored over the last century, it looks today very much as it did in the Middle Ages.

The northern reaches of the City have their own attractions. Close to Liverpool Street Station is Old Spitalfields Market, which, as early as the 11th century, was where you went to buy horses, cattle and pigs. It has recently been restored, and is now packed with market stalls, restaurants and cafés, attracting many visitors. And around the City there are many other flourishing markets with ancient origins, like Petticoat Lane, Leadenhall, Fish Street, Brick Lane and Smithfield.

Just south of London Wall, off Gresham St, is the Guildhall, the centre of City government since the Middle Ages. Its Great Hall was built in the 15th century, and though damaged in the Great Fire in 1666 and during World War II it was beautifully restored by Sir Giles Scott in the 1950s. The Guildhall art gallery contains an fine collection of pre-Raphaelite paintings, and its Clock Museum has one of the finest horoligical displays in the country.

At the western end of London Wall, is the famous Museum of London, and next to it the huge area of Barbican, built over a 40-acre site devastated by World War II bombing and opened in 1982. Here are two theatres, three cinemas, a concert hall, two art galleries, three restaurants and a library, as well as the Guildhall School of Music and Drama, the City of London School for Girls, and 2,014 flats and penthouse apartments.

BELOW
ROYAL COURTS OF JUSTICE
The eastern end of the Strand marks the entrance to legal London, beginning with the impresseive neo-Gothic Law Courts building, and including the four ancient Inns of Court: Lincoln's Inn, the Inner Temple, the Middle Temple (shown below) and Gray's Inn. Members of the public are admitted to the Law Courts' imposing Central Hall, and can attend many of the civil trials held there by sitting in the public galleries.

RIGHT
THE SCALES OF JUSTICE
The Old Bailey, formally known as the Central Criminal Court, at which many of Britain's major criminal trials take place, stands on the site of the historic Newgate Gaol, a place of incarceration for almost 800 years until it finally closed in 1902. The statue above the building, of Justice holding a sword in one hand and a pair of scales in the other, and with a five-pointed star on her head, was sculpted in 1907 by F.W. Pomery.

LEFT

THE BANK OF ENGLAND
Alongside the Royal Exchange in Threadneedle Street (see p.87) is the elegant frontage of the Bank of England, designed by Sir John Soane in 1788. The building is much larger than it appears, covering almost three acres and stretching north to Lothbury. On the eastern side, in Bartholomew Lane, is the entrance to its museum.

BELOW

THE MONUMENT
Another of Sir Christopher Wren's creations is this 202-ft high Doric column on Fish Street Hill, erected in 1677 to commemorate the Great Fire of 1666. A winding 311-step staircase within takes you up to the balcony at the top, providing impressive views around the City.

ST BARTHOLOMEW THE GREAT
Here, tucked away at the southeastern end of
Smithfield Market, is the oldest surviving church
in London, dating from the early 12th century,
when numerous miracles were reported to have
occurred within its walls. They included the
appearance of the Virgin Mary before a lay brother
of the monastery, to whom she declared: "I will
receive their prayers and vows, and will grant them
mercy and blessing for ever."

OVERLEAF, FOLDOUT
THE CITY AT NIGHT
Here we are looking eastward from Tower 42 in Old Broad Street (on the right) toward Canary Wharf, where 1 Canada Square is currently the tallest building in Britain.

LEFT
LLOYD'S OF LONDON
The world's leading insurance market, named after Edward Lloyd's coffee shop (opened in 1688), has a long and impressive history. Today its headquarters are housed in a striking glass and steel edifice at No. 1 Lime Street, designed by Richard Rogers and opened by the Queen in 1986.

RIGHT
ST PAUL'S CATHEDRAL FAÇADE
When Sir Christopher Wren designed the Cathedral after the Great Fire in 1666, he envisaged it as the centre of a new City containing grand squares and broad avenues lined with elegant buildings. But this was not to be, and the area is still surrounded by winding streets and alleys with medieval origins.

FAR LEFT

ALL HALLOWS BARKING

This modest church is situated just a stone's throw from the Tower of London. However, its origins are older than the Tower as the land on which it stands was granted to Barking Abbey by the Bishop of London in 675. Today's church, with its post-war interior and spire, incorporates some earlier incarnations, including fragments of the Norman church that stood on this site almost a thousand years ago.

LEFT

CHRIST CHURCH SPITALFIELDS

This splendid baroque church on the corner of Commercial Street and Fournier Street, designed by Nicholas Hawksmoor and completed in 1729, has recently been beautifully restored at a cost of £10 million, and is now regularly used as a theatre, opera house and concert hall.

LONDON CULTURE

For at least a century London has claimed to be the theatre capital of the world, and although this may be contested, particularly by New York, it does indeed have a long tradition and a wide range of active theatres and productions. The West End contains more than 40 of the main commercial theatres, four of them in Shaftesbury Avenue alone; and the main publicly funded theatre is the Royal National on the South Bank. One of the oldest is the Theatre Royal in Drury Lane, where a theatre has existed since 1663; the present building was designed by Benjamin Wyatt in 1811-12. There are at least 80 major theatres throughout London, and numerous pubs, clubs and halls serving local audiences. The Theatre Museum in Tavistock Street provides a vivid portrayal of theatrical history since Elizabethan times. Many tourists and Londoners alike are attracted to the Globe on Bankside, built in 1997 as a reconstruction of the 16th-century theatre that once lay 200 yards away where Shakespeare performed.

The magnificent Royal Opera House in Covent Garden, the third theatre to exist on this site, was designed by E.M. Barry in 1880 and is today the home of the Royal Opera and Royal Ballet companies. Fine opera, ballet and dance productions also take place at the Coliseum in St Martin's Lane (home of the English National Opera) and Sadler's Wells in Rosebury Avenue, not to mention The Place in Duke's Road, the Rambert Dance Company in Chiswick High Road, and the Peacock Theatre in Kingsway.

London also has many concert halls, including the Royal Albert Hall, a huge amphitheatre with a glass dome on the southern side of Hyde Park, built in 1867-71, where up to 8,000 people can attend concerts, balls, public meetings – and even tennis matches and skating performances. The Royal Festival Hall on the South Bank was built for the Festival of Britain in 1951, and has two neighbouring smaller concert halls, the Purcell Room and Queen Elizabeth Hall. The Barbican's concert hall seats 2,000, and is the headquarters of the London Symphony Orchestra. Another favourite venue for classical music lovers is the Wigmore Hall, built in 1901 by the Bechstein piano company next to their shop in Wigmore Street. Talented young players can be heard at the Royal College of Music in Prince Consort Road and the Royal Academy of Music in Marylebone Road. If jazz, rock and pop music are your preference, there are dozens of live performances every night in clubs, pubs and bars throughout London, and major gigs in such locations as the Astoria in Charing Cross Road, the 100 Club in Oxford Street, Brixton Academy in Stockwell Road, and the Empire in Shepherd's Bush.

Film-going is also a popular activity in London, and after a decline in the 1980s there has been a large increase in the number of general and specialist cinemas throughout the capital. The National Film Theatre, recently refurbished, has been on the South Bank since 1958. It contains four auditoria, a museum, and the headquarters of the British Film Institute, which owns the largest film archive in the world; and this is where the London Film Festival takes place every year in October. Among the more unusual and pleasant privately-owned cinemas are the Electric in Portobello Road, the Curzon in Mayfair and the Tricycle in Kilburn.

London also contains some of the finest art collections in Europe, and has a plethora of commercial art galleries dealing in contemporary art, many of them based in

OPPOSITE

THE BRITISH MUSEUM
The Great Court, at the centre of the British Museum, was originally the location of the British Library's famous Reading Room, until the library was moved to St Pancras in 1990. This impressive, two-acre square in the centre of the museum was designed by Norman Foster and opened by the Queen in December 2000.

LEFT

HER MAJESTY'S THEATRE
The first theatre on this site in the Haymarket, designed by John Vanbrugh, opened in 1705, but it burned down in 1789. The present building, with its Baroque copper dome, was founded by Sir Herbert Tree in 1897.

BELOW

STRAND THEATRE
The Strand Theatre at the western side of Aldwych, by Catherine Street, was opened in 1905 and contains this elegant staircase in the foyer.

and around Cork Street off Piccadilly, or in Portobello Road. The major art auctions take place at Christie's in King Street or Sotheby's in New Bond Street. The best known public collections are at the National Gallery, the National Portrait Gallery, Tate Modern, Tate Britain and the Royal Academy of Arts; but there are many others, such as the Courtauld, Dulwich Picture Gallery, the Saatchi Gallery and the Wallace Collection. Exhibitions are also held at the Hayward Gallery on the South Bank, the Barbican Art Gallery, the ICA Gallery in the Mall, the Queen's Gallery at Buckingham Palace, the Bankside Gallery, the Serpentine Gallery in Kensington Gardens, and many others. Rather more esoteric are such institutions as Leighton House and Linley Sambourne House in Kensington, the William Morris Gallery in Forest Road, and the Iveagh collection in Kenwood House, Hampstead. Large amounts of rather less impressive art are displayed on sale in the open air every Sunday along the south sides of Piccadilly and Bayswater Road.

There are also more than 200 museums around London, covering almost every conceivable subject, from aircraft to zoology, which attract around 30 million visitors every year. Almost a fifth of London's workforce, some 700,000 people, is employed in these cultural and creative sectors. There are museums of clocks, toys, surgery, music, clothes and sport, among many others. The major antiquity collections are to be found at the British Museum and the Victoria and Albert Museum. War is commemorated at the Imperial War Museum, the National Army Museum, the Tower of London, the Cabinet War Rooms, the RAF Museum, and the Guards Museum in Birdcage Walk. Among the best collections covering science and

medicine are the Science Museum, the Natural History Museum, and the Faraday Museum. More arcane collections include the Fan Museum in Greenwich, the Florence Nightingale Museum in Lambeth Palace Road, the Ragged School Museum in Copperfield Road, and the London Dungeon in Tooley Street. Among the most popular is Madame Tussaud's in Marylebone Road. There are also a number of interesting former private houses open to the public in memory of their inhabitants, such as Sigmund Freud, the Duke of Wellington, Samuel Johnson, Sir John Soane, John Keats, George Frideric Handel, Thomas Carlyle and Charles Dickens.

If you want to know where famous Londoners lived in the past, there is a long tradition of erecting "blue plaques" on their homes, a system first introduced in 1867. They are selected by public vote, and curiously a number of past celebrities, such as Sir Thomas More and Sir Isaac Newton, have not been included. But there are many hundreds to be found, more than 90 in the borough of Kensington and Chelsea alone. You can find George Eliot in Cheyne Walk, A.A. Milne in Mallord Street, Mark Twain in Tedworth Square and James Joyce in Campden Grove.

RIGHT
SHAKESPEARE'S GLOBE
Inspired and organized by the late American actor and film-maker Sam Wanamaker, the Globe is a meticulous reconstruction of the Tudor open-air theatre in which Shakespeare performed many of his plays at the beginning of the 17th century. The original theatre was located nearby in Park Street, and was demolished in 1644.

OPPOSITE
PALACE THEATRE
Cambridge Circus, half way up Charing Cross Road, is not a pretty square, but it is dominated by the impressive terracotta façade of Palace Theatre, designed by T.E. Colcutt in 1888. Throughout the 1990s the theatre staged the hugely successful musical production of Les Misérables.

ABOVE
FLORAL HALL
One of the attractions of the Royal Opera House is the recently restored Floral Hall, at the southern end of the building. It was first opened in 1860, and is now used as a bar and restaurant – and even for tea-time dancing.

RIGHT
THE ROYAL OPERA HOUSE
At the eastern end of Covent Garden, on Bow Street, the impressive Royal Opera House is the home of the Royal Ballet and the Royal Opera companies. Its magnificent auditorium, decorated in white and gold, seats 2,158 people.

ABOVE
ABOVE
THE ROYAL ALBERT HALL
On Kensington Gore, opposite the Albert Memorial, this immense amphitheatre with extraordinary acoustics can hold an audience of up to 8,000. It is perhaps most famous for its annual series of summer classical concerts known as "The Proms".

LEFT
SADLER'S WELLS
At the northern end of Rosebury Avenue, stands the striking, modern Sadler's Wells theatre, on a site where music halls have existed since the late 17th century. It is a major location for ballet and popular dance productions.

NATURAL HISTORY MUSEUM

On Cromwell Road, the Natural History Museum dominates the southern end of "museumland", with its grandiose Romanesque-style frontage designed by Alfred Waterhouse in 1873-80. It contains a magnificent national collection covering zoology, botany, paleontology, entomology, geology and mineralogy, and now also includes many interactive exhibits. The impressive dinosaur skeletons (shown opposite) are the first of the museum's inhabitants to greet visitors in its grand entrance hall.

THE VICTORIA AND ALBERT MUSEUM

On the other side of Exhibition Road is the V&A, containing what has been described as the finest collection of applied art and design in the world. Originally launched by Queen Victoria as the South Kensington Museum and School, the present building, designed by Sir Aston Webb, was opened in 1909. Among the huge range of collections one of the most popular is the Costume Court, showing English and European fashionable clothes from around 1580 to the present day.

TRAFALGAR SQUARE

With the National Gallery at the northern end, and dominated by Nelson's Column, Trafalgar Square is traditionally the main London location for public protests, demonstrations and New Year celebrations. In this view the building seen on the left is Canada House, dating from 1824; and on the right lies the National Gallery, where much of the nation's fine art collection is displayed. In the foreground is one of the square's impressive fountains, which are attractively lit at night.

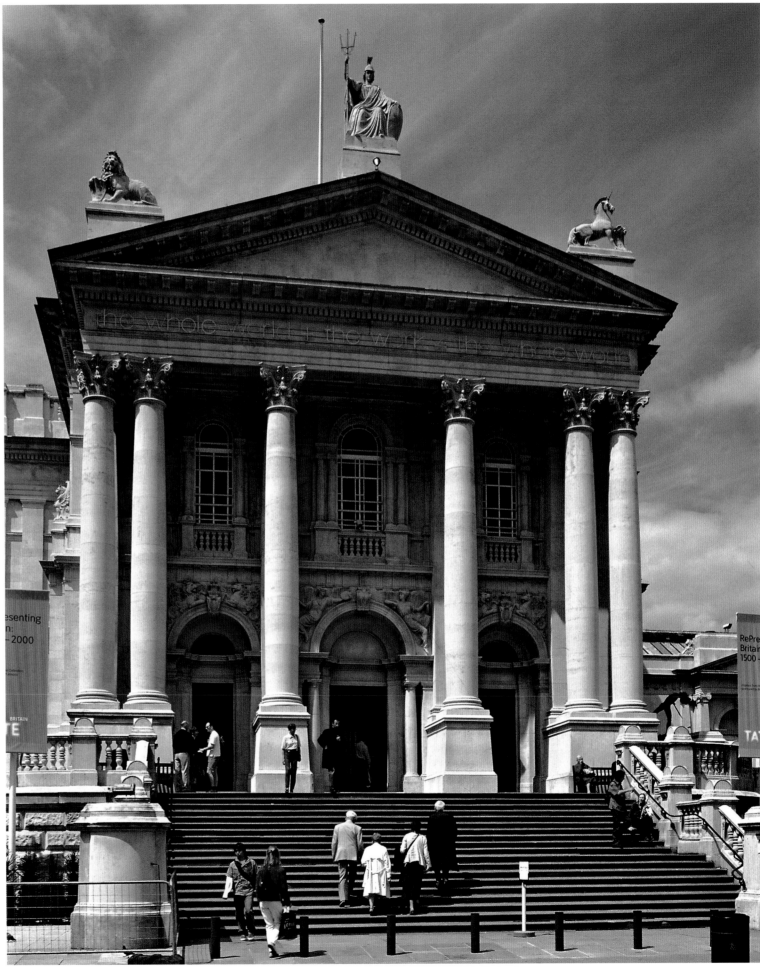

TATE MODERN
In the year 2000 the vast Bankside Power Station building across the river from St Paul's Cathedral was converted into Tate Modern, to house the national collection of contemporary art. It has proved extremely popular with both Londoners and tourists alike.

BRITISH MUSEUM
There is no richer or more varied collection in the world than that of the British Museum in Bloomsbury. Fronted by the imposing classical façade and portico on the south side, it contains 94 permanent and temporary exhibition galleries.

IMPERIAL WAR MUSEUM
This fine collection covering 20th-century conflicts is housed in a grand building in Lambeth which was once the Bethlehem Royal Hospital, dating back to 1247, and known to Londoners as Bedlam.

TATE BRITAIN
This neo-classical building on Millbank is the home of the national collection of British paintings, and includes the Clore Gallery which houses the J.M.W. Turner collection. The restaurant on the western side is famous for its cuisine and wine list.

ROYAL ACADEMY
Off Piccadilly, the quadrangle in front of Burlington House, home of the Royal Academy of Arts, also contains various other learned organizations, such as the Linnean Society, the Geological Society and the Society of Antiquaries. The RA's Summer Exhibition, showing works by contemporary amateur and professional artists, is a popular annual event.

CABINET WAR ROOMS
As a memorial to Britain's valour in World War II, 19 underground rooms in Horse Guards Road have been preserved just as they were when the war ended in 1945. They include the Cabinet Room, Churchill's bedroom, and the Map Room (above).

RIGHT
SIR JOHN SOANE'S MUSEUM
Sir John Soane (1753-1837), architect of the Bank of England and Dulwich Picture Gallery, lived at 13 Lincoln's Inn Fields, and bequeathed his house and its remarkable art collections to the nation. It still conveys the atmosphere of an early 19th-century private home, and contains a fascinating range of antiques, furniture and works of art, including two series of fine paintings by William Hogarth, the *Rake's Progress* and the *Election*.

OPPOSITE
THE QUEEN'S GALLERY
The southern end of Buckingham Palace was severely damaged in World War II, and was rebuilt in the 1960s. The western part was turned into the Queen's Gallery, which regularly exhibits splendid art and artifacts from the impressive Royal Collection, accumulated by Britain's monarchs over several centuries.

LONDON LIFE

The 609 square miles that comprise Greater London contain a population of about 7½ million people, and its enormous cultural diversity and the plethora of ethnic-minority communities – almost 2½ million people – make it one of the most fascinating and stimulating cities in the world. One quarter of all British unemployed men and women live in London, and three of Britain's five most deprived boroughs are based here, but there is also immense affluence. In 2003 the cost of living was reported to be the seventh highest in the world, and the third highest in Europe after Moscow and Geneva. The notably high costs are for property, accommodation, transport, alcohol and tobacco. In 2004 the average rent for a one-bedroom flat was between £600 and £700 per month, the average weekly grocery bill, £60; and most workers spend £70 a month travelling. These costs can be reduced by more than a third throughout the rest of Britain, so life is not necessarily easy for Londoners.

Transport around London has been a problem over several centuries. Bus services were first introduced in 1829, and by 1900 the thousands of buses were carrying 50 million passengers a year. Double-deckers, originally with their upper decks open to the air, first appeared in 1909, and are still much used today. Indeed London's red double-decker buses are one of the most iconic symbols of the capital. Taxis date back to 1834, when Joseph Hansom invented the hansom-cab, a light, four-wheeled carriage drawn by a horse. The motor-driven version was introduced in 1903, and London Taxis International, the leading manufacturer, has produced over 100,000 of their current TX1 and TX2 models. The underground railways began in the 1860s, and the electrified "tubes" in 1905; and today there are more than 100 miles of tube lines across London. But Londoners are far from committed to travelling by public transport: most of the main streets are packed all day with bicycles, motorbikes, cars, vans and trucks. The introduction, in 2003, of congestion charging in the central area has alleviated this, but at the cost of undermining the retail industry within the zone.

Shopping is a favourite activity for Londoners, and in Oxford Street, one of the largest and most popular shopping areas, retailers claimed in 2004 to have lost £300 million in trade since congestion charging began. This is where great superstores like Selfridges, John Lewis, Marks & Spencer and Topshop are located. Supermarkets are dotted all over the city, and there are specialist areas such as fashion clothes around Great Portland Street and furniture in King's Road. Open-air markets are also a growing feature, although some of their origins date back as far as the almost a thousand years. For example, Billingsgate was already thriving in 1016, selling wine, salt, pottery, corn, coal and fish. Some of the most popular markets today include Borough Market in Southwark, Brick Lane, Camden Lock Market and the London Farmers' Market in Notting Hill Gate.

In the first half of the last century, Britain was famous for its poor cooking and third-rate eating places, but over recent decades this has changed dramatically. There are now many Michelin-starred restaurants, and as wide a range of cuisines as can be imagined, from Afghan to Vietnamese. A prototype of this huge variety is Upper Street in Islington, where there is currently a whole range of restaurants offering different kinds of food. So many Londoners now eat out that there are worries that home cooking skills are in decline.

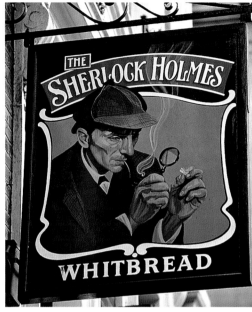

OPPOSITE, TOP LEFT
TURNBULL & ASSER
Jermyn Street, running parallel to Piccadilly, was called after the Earl of St Albans' family name, and contains an attractive range of fashionable gentlemen's clothes shops.

OPPOSITE, BOTTOM LEFT
GIEVES & HAWKES
At one time Savile Row was famously the street where gentlemen went for their bespoke, tailored suits and morning coats. Gieves & Hawkes, at the southern end, still provides this service.

OPPOSITE, TOP RIGHT AND BOTTOM RIGHT
JERMYN STREET
Although much of Jermyn Street is devoted to men's clothes shops, there are exceptions. Paxton & Whitfield at number 93 provides a high-class delicatessen; and Floris, who sell unguents and perfumes, are at number 89.

ABOVE
THE SHERLOCK HOLMES
Fans of Sir Arthur Conan Doyle's Sherlock Holmes can enjoy the museum dedicated to the eccentric detective at 221B Baker Street, just south of Regent's Park; but this pub is to be found in Northumberland Street, behind Charing Cross Station.

LEFT AND ABOVE LEFT
TAXIS AND SHOPPING BAGS
London's characteristic black cabs are a useful, if more expensive, way to travel around the city. The shopper who has just left the famous toystore Hamleys, in Regent Street, clearly needs one.

115

A recent survey by leading food experts of the world's best restaurants nominated eight London venues in their top 50.

As long as 700 years ago there were already more than 350 taverns in London, and by 1870 the number of public houses and beer shops had risen to 20,000. Most of these still survive, some with much older histories, and this is where vast numbers of Londoners go to meet with friends and relax after the working day. And like London's restaurants they have much improved in recent decades, offering not only a decent range of beers, lagers and wines, but live music and dancing, upstairs theatres, and even respectable food. According to a recent survey, London offers many of the very best pubs in Britain, including the George Inn in Southwark, with its large open courtyard and numerous bars; Jerusalem Tavern in Clerkenwell, originally opened in the 1720s, and popular for its St Peters Brewery ales; and The Lamb in Bloomsbury, which is also 18th century in origin. My own favourite is the Anglesey Arms in Hammersmith.

One notable advance in modern London is the rapidly growing popularity of gyms and fitness clubs, many hundreds of which have opened around the capital in recent years, not only in residential areas but also in the City and the West End. Some are run by international chains, some are managed by borough councils, and many are privately owned. A code of practice has been developed by the Fitness Industry Association, and most of these places offer, in addition to gym equipment, a wide range of yoga, pilates and other classes, swimming pools, tennis and squash courts, and personal medical check-ups. This tendency may well indicate that the health of Londoners, which over the last millennium has been notoriously poor, is likely to improve.

If sport is your interest, London has much to offer here too. The most popular, as it is throughout Britain, is football, which Londoners have certainly played since early Medieval times. The London football clubs of Arsenal and Chelsea are world-class, but West Ham United, Tottenham Hotspur, Queen's Park Rangers and Charlton Athletic are just as popular with their fans. Cricket has at least as long a history, and world cricket, run by the International Cricket Council, is still based at Lord's Cricket Ground in St John's Wood. Rugby Union, the sport in which England became world champions in 2003, has its headquarters at Twickenham. Many other sports are a traditional part of London life, including boxing, skateboarding, rowing – and of course tennis. Amateur tennis players, footballers, cricketers and rugby players can perform their sport all over the parks and green spaces. The All England Lawn Tennis Club in Wimbledon stages the most famous annual tennis championships in the world.

OPPOSITE, LEFT
LONDON BUSES ON OXFORD STREET
The red double-decker Routemaster bus, with a distinctive open entrance at the rear, was introduced in 1956. However, this style of bus is now slowly being phased out in favour of more modern designs. Most private vehicles are banned from driving down London's busy Oxford Street during the day – hence the common sight of the street being filled end-to-end with buses and taxis.

OPPOSITE, RIGHT
ST PANCRAS
Completed in 1872, the astonishing, high-Gothic-style St Pancras Station, was originally a luxurious 25-bedroom hotel, but this closed in 1935. The hotel is being refurbished, and is expected to be finished by 2008. The hotel will become private apartments, with the lower rooms as restaurants and bars.

LEFT
CHRISTMAS LIGHTS
In the West End over the Christmas season, the retailers in Oxford Street and Regent Street (shown here) fund elaborate lighting to encourage their customers to come and spend.

ABOVE
LONDON UNDERGROUND SIGN
The London underground's distinctive logo is seen here outside Leicester Square station, just off the Charing Cross Road.

117

RIGHT, TOP
CARNABY STREET
In the 1960s Carnaby Street was the mecca for teenage pop and fashion. It has recently been refurbished, and is now a pedestrian shopping area, running south from Great Marlborough Street to Beak Street.

RIGHT, BOTTOM
LIBERTY
This distinguished department store is divided in two parts, with a frontage on Regent's Street, and a 1920s mock-Tudor building with a St-George-and-the-Dragon clock on Great Marlborough Street.

FAR RIGHT
CECIL COURT
Running between Charing Cross Road and St Martin's Lane, Cecil Court is full of attractive second-hand bookshops. Mozart once lodged here in 1764.

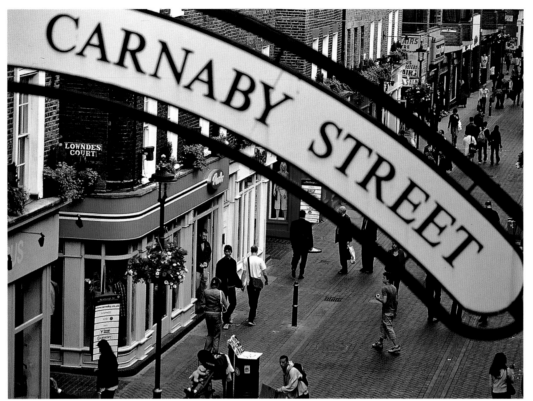

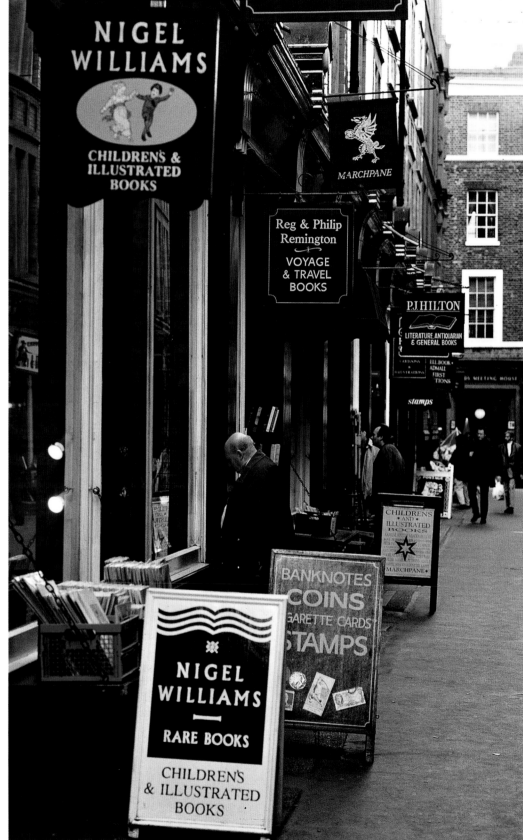

HARRODS
In 1849 a small grocery store in Brompton Road, run by Henry Charles Harrod, began to expand rapidly, and by the end of the century it already claimed to "serve the world". Today Harrods is Britain's largest department store, occupying a four-acre site in Knightsbridge. The food halls on the ground floor, designed between 1901 and 1905 by Stevens and Munt, are particularly impressive.

PICCADILLY CIRCUS AT NIGHT
Situated at the junction of five busy London streets, in the heart of the capital's theatreland, Piccadilly Circus has long been a famous landmark, with its bright neon advertisements and popular small statue of a winged archer (shown here on the far right), known to all as Eros – the god of love.

LEFT
LEADENHALL MARKET
Some of London's markets date back past the Middle Ages, but Leadenhall is comparatively modern – it was the place to buy poultry and cheese in the 14th century. Today's beautiful buildings were designed by Horace Jones in 1881, and though badly damaged by a terrorist assault in 1992 they have been elegantly restored. They still include meat-and-game traders, as well as coffee shops and bars.

RIGHT
BURLINGTON ARCADE
Running north from Piccadilly alongside the Royal Academy, Burlington Arcade is a long and elegant pedestrian passage lined on either side with mahogany-fronted shops selling fashionable goods. Lord Cavendish (later to become the Earl of Burlington) built it in 1818, originally to stop passers-by from throwing rubbish into his garden next door.